# THE AZTEC

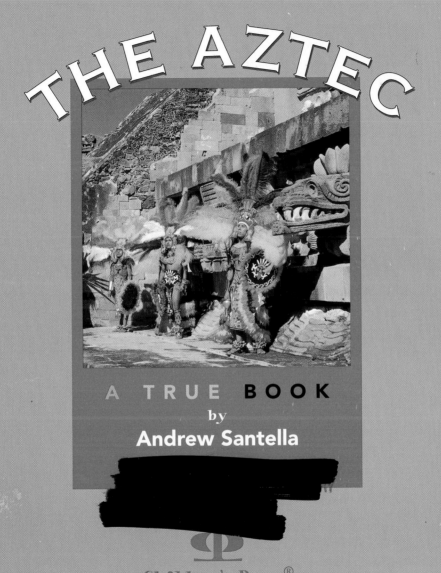

## A TRUE BOOK

by

**Andrew Santella**

**Children's Press®**
A Division of Scholastic Inc.

New York  Toronto  London  Auckland  Sydney
Mexico City  New Delhi  Hong Kong
Danbury, Connecticut

Aztec dancer

*Reading Consultant*
**Nanci R. Vargus, Ed.D.**
*Primary Multiage Teacher*
*Decatur Township Schools*
*Indianapolis, IN*

*Content Consultant*
**Dr. Ruth J. Krochock**
*Archaeologist*
*Davis, California*

*The photograph on the cover shows an Aztec boy in a leopard costume. The photograph on the title page shows Aztec dancers in native costums.*

Library of Congress Cataloging-in-Publication Data

Santella, Andrew.
    The Aztec / by Andrew Santella.
        p. cm. – (A True book)
    Includes bibliographical references and index.
    Summary: Describes the Aztec way of life, including their religion, society, capital city, and government.
        ISBN 0-516-22500-6 (lib. bdg.)    0-516-26973-9 (pbk.)
    1. Aztecs—Juvenile literature. [1. Aztecs. 2. Indians of Mexico.] I. Title. II. Series.
F1219.73.S29 2002
972'.018—dc21                                                    2001032302

CHILDREN'S PRESS, AND A TRUE BOOK®, and associated logos are trademarks and or registered trademarks of Grolier Publishing Co., Inc. SCHOLASTIC and associated logos are trademarks and or registered trademarks of Scholastic Inc.

1 2 3 4 5 6 7 8 9 10 R 11 10 09 08 07 06 05 04 03 02

# Contents

The Aztec ... 5

The Aztec Capital ... 9

Religion ... 21

Farming ... 29

Society and Government ... 34

The Spanish Conquest ... 38

To Find Out More ... 44

Important Words ... 46

Index ... 47

Meet the Author ... 48

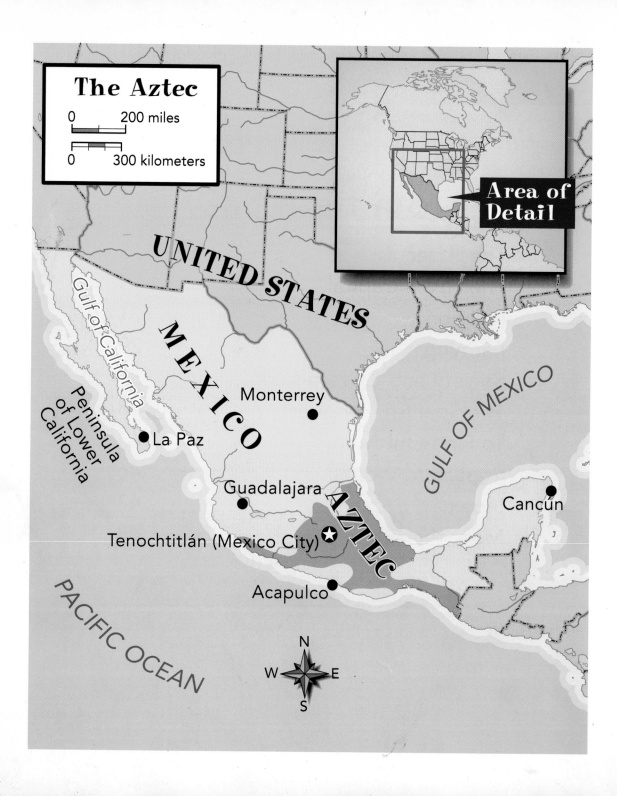

**The Aztec**

0  200 miles

0  300 kilometers

Area of Detail

UNITED STATES

MEXICO

Gulf of California

Peninsula of Lower California

Monterrey

La Paz

GULF OF MEXICO

Guadalajara

AZTEC

Cancún

Tenochtitlán (Mexico City)

Acapulco

PACIFIC OCEAN

N
W    E
S

# The Aztec

About eight hundred years ago, a group of people called the Mexica (may-SHEE-ka) began moving away from their homeland in northern Mexico. Sometime in the 1200s, they moved to a valley hundreds of miles to the south. There they built a great city. Today, that valley is home to one of the world's largest cities—Mexico City.

When they arrived, the Mexica found other people already living in the valley. The other people lived on the best, most fertile land. The Mexica had to make do with the land that no one else wanted, and they struggled to survive in their new home.

However, the Mexica did have a skill that served them

well. They were fierce warriors. In the many wars that were fought for control of the valley, everyone wanted the Mexica as allies. As a result, the Mexica became one of the most powerful groups in the valley. Eventually, they joined forces with two other peoples—the Tepaneca (te-pan-E-ka) and the Acolhuaca (a-kol-WA-ka). These three groups formed the Triple Alliance. Together, they began building a vast **empire**

centered in the valley. Today we call the people of that empire the Aztec.

# The Aztec Capital

The Aztec ruled the greatest empire in Mexican history. At one point, it covered more than 80,000 square miles (207,200 square kilometers). That is about the size of Utah! At one point the Aztec ruled over more than 12 million people.

9

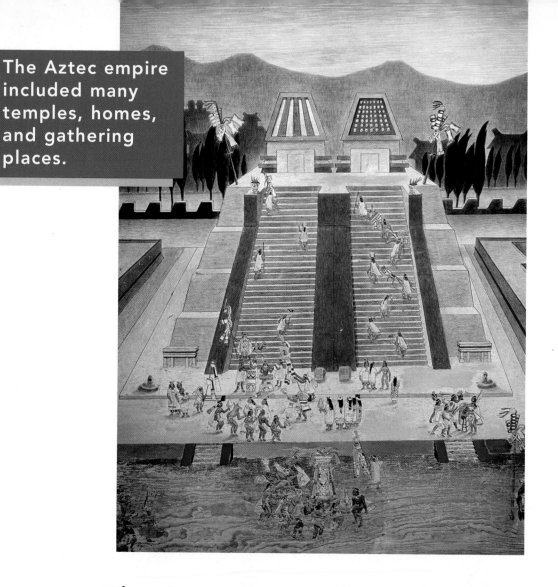

The Aztec empire began with the building of the city of Tenochtitlán (te-noch-TEE-tlan).

The Aztec believed that one of their gods had given them instructions on where to build their city. They believed that their god had promised to

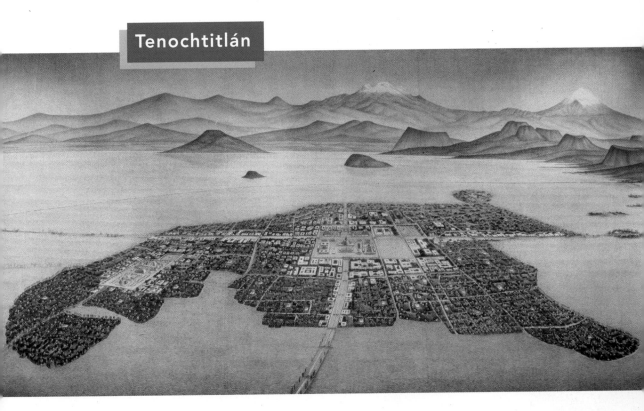

Tenochtitlán

The Aztec believed that an eagle on a cactus with a serpent in its beak was a sign from the gods.

send them a sign. If they saw an eagle perched on a cactus holding a **serpent** in its beak, it would be a sign from their god to settle in that spot. According to Aztec legend, they saw just such a sight on a **marshy** island in the middle of Lake Texcoco (tesh-KO-ko). They began building their city there sometime around 1325.

The island in the lake was a difficult place to build a city. As Tenochtitlán grew, the Aztec had to fill in parts of the lake

The Aztec were constantly filling in the lake to use it for building and farming.

with soil to make more room on which to build. Then they had to build huge and complicated waterworks to bring fresh water to the city. Nevertheless, the Aztec lived well in Tenochtitlán.

A king named Itzacoatl (eets-a-KO-atl) led the building of Tenochtitlán. He built temples and roads. He even built a bridge across the lake. Itzacoatl also began leading the Aztec on wars of conquest.

Itzacoatl built a bridge across Lake Texcoco.

Montezuma led the Aztec on many conquests.

He was followed by King Montezuma I (mon-te-SOO-ma), who led the Aztec on even more conquests. As the Aztec won more wars, Tenochtitlán grew larger and more spectacular. The Aztec built temples that were larger than the ones before. They cut canals through the island.

The Aztec built many spectacular temples in Tenochtitlán.

They built markets that they filled with products and people. The city was becoming the **capital** of a great empire.

The Aztec were almost always at war. Aztec victories in war

helped to make their empire richer and grander. The tribute they collected from defeated enemies helped support the growing Aztec society. Defeated people paid the Aztec in food, clothing, gold, honey, and even colorful birds' feathers. As the Aztec became more powerful, other people had no choice but to pay to support the Aztec empire. If they resisted, they would be killed.

# The Image Lives On

tenochtitlan

The Aztec legend of the eagle and the cactus lives on in Mexico. Mexico's flag features an image of an eagle with a snake in its beak that is perched on a cactus.

The images of an eagle and a cactus are common in Aztec art (above). The Mexican flag (left) still depicts the ancient Aztec image.

# Religion

The Aztec believed in thousands of gods, some of which were more important than others. The Aztec calendar was filled with special days honoring these gods. They also built temples to honor their gods. The greatest Aztec temple was called

Templo Mayor. Located in
Tenochtitlán, it was 200 feet
(61 meters) tall.

One of the most important
Aztec gods controlled the sun
and war. This god was called

Huitzilopochtli (wee-tsee-lo-POCH-tlee). The Aztec believed that he made the sun rise each day. The Aztec also believed that Huitzilopochtli and the

Huitzilopochtli, an Aztec god of sun and war

other gods would only favor them if the Aztec continued to give them gifts. So the Aztec offered the gods gifts of food. They also performed athletic contests in honor of the gods. The Aztec believed that the most powerful gift of all was the gift of a living human heart.

The Aztec captured many prisoners during the wars. They killed some of these prisoners and offered their hearts as presents to the Aztec gods.

Temple of the Sun

Such a present was called a sacrifice. One of the reasons the Aztec started wars was to capture prisoners to be killed and sacrificed to the gods. The Aztec sometimes sacrificed hundreds and thousands of victims at one time. One Aztec ruler is believed to have ordered 20,000 prisoners of war killed in a single ceremony.

Although the Aztec may be remembered for their human sacrifices, that was only one part of their religion. The Aztec borrowed many of their religious beliefs from other people, including some from the peoples they conquered. The Aztec divided the history

of their people into ages or "suns." Each sun lasted 2,028 years. They believed that there had been four suns since the creation of the world. Each sun ended in a disaster that wiped out all the people. When the

The Aztec believed that Tonatiuh ruled the "sun" they lived in.

empire was at its largest, the Aztec believed they were in the fifth sun. They believed that this period was controlled by a sun god called Tonatiuh (to-na-TEE-yooh).

# Farming

One of the keys to the success of the Aztec empire was its system of **agriculture.** Agriculture is the growing of crops for food. The Aztec made the most of whatever land was available. They dug ditches that carried water from rivers to dry land. They

The Aztec learned how to fill in marshes to use for farming.

filled in **swamps** and marshes to use them for farming. The Aztec managed to grow many good crops on land that other people might not have bothered trying to farm.

The Aztec even managed to farm on Lake Texcoco. They laid reeds down in the shallow parts of the lake and covered them with soil. Then they grew crops in the soil. Eventually, the Aztec were able to use much of the lake for farming. More than half of the people of Tenochtitlán made their living as farmers.

Aztec farming methods helped make their empire rich. The vegetables that the Aztecs

Corn (left) and tomatoes (above) were important crops for the Aztecs.

grew became the main part of their diet. They grew corn, beans, squash, and tomatoes. They also ate the creatures that lived in and around Lake Texcoco—snails, fish, turtles, and frogs.

# Aztec Picture Writing

**T**he Aztec spoke a language called Nahuatl (na-WA-tl). There were no letters used to write down Nahuatl. The Aztec used symbols and pictures to represent things and ideas when writing their language.

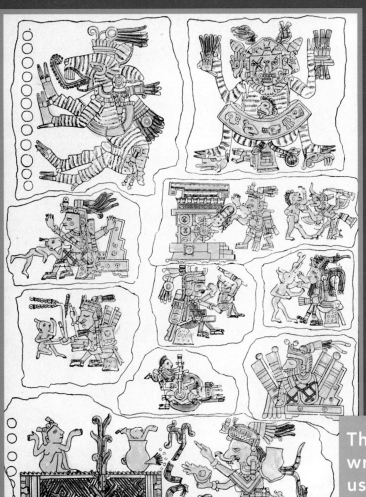

The Aztec used picture writing instead of using written words.

# Society and Government

Aztec society was divided into **nobles** and **commoners**. Nobles were wealthy people of high rank. Commoners were ordinary people. However, even a very poor commoner could rise to become a noble. One way to move up in Aztec society was to show great skill in warfare.

The nicer homes in Tenochtitlán belonged to nobles.

Nobles lived in large adobe homes that had courtyards in the centers. Adobe is a brick made from straw and mud that is dried in the sun. Commoners lived in huts made of clay or dried grasses spread over a wood frame.

Many Aztec people owned slaves. A person became a slave if he was unable to pay off his debts or if he was captured in battle.

Aztec government was headed by the emperor, or "chief of men." He was supported by warriors, ambassadors, high priests, and judges. The empire contained fifty to sixty city-states. Sometimes, rulers of people conquered by the Aztec were allowed to continue ruling their people. However, they had to pay tribute to the Aztec emperor and serve as part of the Aztec empire.

Only men were allowed to become high priests in Aztec society.

Women did not have the same opportunities as men did in Aztec society. Many jobs in government and religion were open only to men. Aztec boys went to school, but girls did not.

# The Spanish Conquest

In 1519, a Spanish force led by Hernán Cortés arrived in Mexico. The Aztec welcomed the Spanish and presented Cortés with gifts. When the Spanish first saw Tenochtitlán, they were amazed at the grand city. "Some of our soldiers even asked whether the

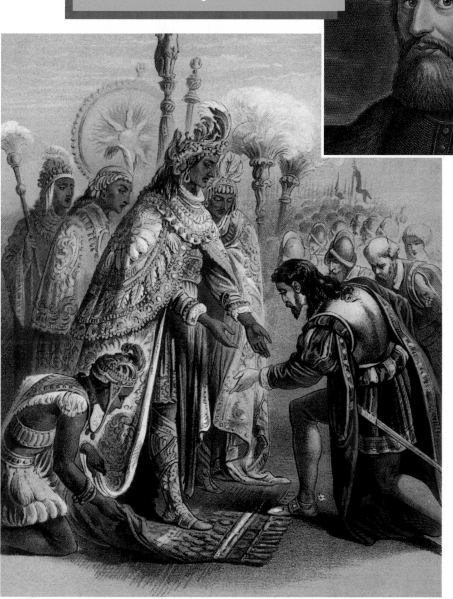

Spanish explorer Hernán Cortés (right); At first, the Aztec welcomed Cortes into their city (below).

things we saw were not a dream," one Spainard wrote.

Cortés was determined to conquer the Aztec. His soldiers were armed with cannons and muskets. The Aztec were armed with razor-sharp knives made of volcanic glass called obsidian. The Spanish horses and large dogs frightened the Aztec. They had never seen such animals. Their superior weapons gave the Spanish a great advantage over the

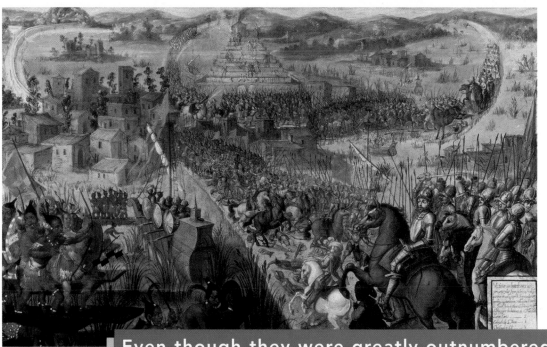

Even though they were greatly outnumbered, the Spanish defeated the Aztec.

Aztec. The Spanish were greatly outnumbered, but they defeated the Aztec.

By 1522 the Aztec empire had crumbled. Spain took control of the land the Aztec once ruled. Under the rule of the Spanish, the Aztec were not allowed to practice their religion or observe their customs. The Spanish destroyed Aztec temples. They made Aztec prisoners work for them as slaves. The Aztec way of life quickly disappeared. So did the Aztec capital, Tenochtitlán. Mexico City, the modern capital of Mexico, grew up in its place. It was built on the very site of the capital of the vast Aztec empire.

Today the capital of Mexico has tall skyscrapers and modern buildings (top). These Aztec dancers participate in a festival in Mexico City (bottom).

# To Find Out More

Here are some additional resources to help you learn more about the Aztec:

 **Books**

Kimmel, Eric A. **The Two Mountains: An Aztec Legend.** Holiday House, 2000.

McDermott, Gerald. **Musicians of the Sun.** Simon and Schuster, 1997.

Patent, Dorothy Hinshaw. **Quetzal: Sacred Bird of the Cloud Forest**. William Morrow and Company, 1996.

Platt, Richard. **Aztecs.** DK Publishing, 1999.

Sherrow, Victoria. **The Aztec Indians.** Chelsea House, 1993.

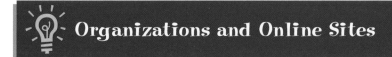

## Organizations and Online Sites

### Aztec Creation Story
*www.Indians.org/welker/*
*aztecs.htm*

Read a common Aztec myth.

### Ancient Mesoamerican Civilization
*www.angelfire.com/ca/*
*humanorigins*

Learn more about the Aztec government and writing system.

### Organization of the Aztec Empire
*www.elbalero.gob.mx/kids/*
*history/html/conquista/*
*imperio.html*

Find out more about Aztec conquests and Tenochtitlán.

# Important Words

*agriculture* the raising of crops, farming

*capital* a city that is home to the government of a state or nation

*commoner* one of the common people; not a person of high rank

*empire* a group of nations or people ruled by a single leader or government

*marsh* a piece of low, wet land

*noble* a person of high rank

*serpent* a snake

*swamp* a piece of wet, spongy land, not fit for farming

# Index

(**Boldface** page numbers
indicate illustrations.)

Acolhuaca, 7
bridge, 14, **15**
calendar, 21, **27**
city-state, 36
commoners, 34, 35
corn, 32, **32**
Cortés, Hernán, 38, **39,**
    40
dogs, 40
eagle, 12, **12,** 20
emperor, 36
empire, **4,** 8, 10, **10,** 18,
    19, 28, 29, 31, 36, 41
farming, 29-32
flag, 20, **20**
food, 19, 24, 29
gods, 11, 12, 21, 22, 23,
    24, 25, 28
government, 34–37
high priests, 36, **37**
homes, **10,** 35, **35**
horses, 40
Huitzilopochtli, 23, **23**
Itzacoatl, 14, 15
Lake Texcoco, 13, **15,** 31,
    32
language, 33

legends, 12, 20
markets, 18, **18**
men, 37
Mexica, 5, 6, 7
Mexico, 5, 6, 9, 20, 38,
    42, **43**
Montezuma, 16, **16**
nobles, 34, 35
prisoners, 24, 25, 26, 42
religion, 21–28, 37, 42
sacrifice, 25, 26
school, 37
slaves, 36, 42
Spanish conquest, 38–42
sun, 22, 23, 27, 28
temples, **10,** 14, 17, **17,**
    21, 22, **22, 25,** 42
Tenochtitlán, 10, **11,** 13,
    14, 16, **17,** 22, 31, **35,**
    38, 42
Tepaneca, 7
tomatoes, 32, **32**
Tonatiuh, 28, **28**
tribute, 19, 36
war, 14, 16, 18, 22, 23,
    24, 25, 26, 34
warriors, 7, 36
weapons, 40
women, 37
writing, 33, **33**

# Meet the Author

Andrew Santella writes for *Gentlemen's Quarterly, the New York Times Book Review*, and other publications. He is also the author of several Children's Press titles.